Artists in Their World

Jackson Pollock

Clare Oliver

W

FRANKLIN WATTS
LONDON•SYDNEY

For Amy and Fionnuala

This edition 2005

First published in 2003 by
Franklin Watts, 338 Euston Road
London NW1 3BH

Franklin Watts Australia
Hachette Children's Books
Level 17/207 Kent St
Sydney NSW 2000

© Franklin Watts 2003

Series Editor: Adrian Cole
Editor: Mary-Jane Wilkins
Series Designer: Mo Choy
Art Director: Jonathan Hair
Picture Researcher: Julie McMahon

A CIP catalogue record for this book
is available from the British Library.

ISBN 0 7496 6649 8

Printed in China

Acknowledgements

AKG London: p11 Going West, 1934-38 © ARS, NY and DACS, London 2003;
p24t; p39 Portrait and a Dream, 1953 © ARS, NY and DACS, London 2003. Art Institute of Chicago: p27 The
Key, 1946 © ARS, NY and DACS, London 2003. Bridgeman / Musee National d'Art Moderne, Paris: cover & p21
Moon Woman Cuts the Circle, 1943 © ARS, NY and DACS, London 2003; Bridgeman / Private Collection p7b;
Bridgeman Giraudon / Lauros / Private Collection p8 Untitled Self Portrait c.1931-35 © ARS, NY and DACS,
London; Bridgeman / Archives Larousse, Paris p14b. Corbis: p10t Bettmann; 14t Abstract Human Figure, 1938
Burstein Collection / © ARS, NY and DACS, London 2003; p16b Composition No.8, 1939-42 © Piet Mondrian
2003 Mondrian/Holtzmann Trust c/o Beeldrecht, Hoofddorp & DACS London; p18t; p18b Harlequin's Carnival,
1924-25 © Succession Miro / DACS, 2003; p24b; p35b; p38b. Culver Pictures: p9b. Hulton / Archive: p10b; p12t;
p16t; p17b; p20t; p28. Magnum Photos: p36 b; p41b. Metropolitian Museum of Modern Art, New York: p25 War
c.1944-46 © ARS, NY and DACS, London 2003. Museo Nacional Centro de Arte Reina Sofia, Madrid /
Bridgeman: p22 Guernica, 1937 © Succession Picasso/DACS, London 2003. Pollock-Krasner House and Study
Center: p6; p7t; p9t; p12b; Museum of Modern Art, NY p19 Stenographic Figure, c.1942 © ARS, NY and DACS,
London 2003; p20 b; Museum of Modern Art, NY p23 The She-Wolf, 1943 © ARS, NY and DACS, London
2003; p26 t & b; p28 t; p30t & b; p31 © Estate of Hans Namuth; p32 c; p32 b © Estate of Hans Namuth; p36t;
p38t; p40. Popperfoto: p17t. Tate Picture Library: p13 Untitled (Naked Man with a Knife), 1938-40 © ARS, NY
and DACS, London 2003; p15 Birth, c.1938-41 © ARS, NY and DACS, London 2003; p34 Eve, 1950 © ARS,
NY and DACS, London 2003; p35 t Untitled, c.1951-2 © Kate Rothko Prizel and Christopher Rothko / DACS
1998; p37 Number 14, 1951 © ARS, NY and DACS, London 2003; p41 Julian Schnabel 'Humanity Asleep' 1982
© ARS, NY and DACS, London 2003. Scala: p29 Full Fathom Five, 1947 © ARS, NY and DACS, London 2003;
p33 No 1a, 1948 © ARS, NY and DACS, London 2003. Syracuse University, NY: p43.

Whilst every attempt has been made to clear copyright
should there be any inadvertent omission please apply
in the first instance to the publisher regarding rectification.

Contents

Who was Jackson Pollock?

▲ The Pollock family enjoying watermelons in Phoenix, Arizona, c.1914-15.
From left to right: Roy, Frank, Charles, Jackson, Jay, Sande and Stella.

Jackson Pollock was one of the first art superstars. He was the leading Abstract Expressionist, one of a group of United States-based artists who found success in the late 1940s.

Pollock's method of splattering paint on to canvas earned him the nickname Jack the Dripper. Amazingly, the drip paintings that made his reputation were all created within a few, busy years.

EARLY LIFE

Nothing in Pollock's boyhood hinted at his future. His parents were of Scottish-Irish descent, and struggled to make a living. Pollock was their fifth and last son, and he was born in Cody, Wyoming on 28 January 1912. Pollock often mentioned his birthplace in interviews, although the family left Cody when he was ten months old. The town was named after 'Buffalo Bill' Cody and stood for all that was wild about the Western frontier – lawlessness, freedom and opportunity.

TIMELINE ▶

1912	1916	1920	1922	1928
Pollock is born in Cody, Wyoming.	Pollock loses a fingertip while chopping wood.	Pollock's father moves away.	Charles enrols at the Otis Art Institute, Los Angeles.	Pollock enrols at Manual Arts High School.

RESTLESS, ROOTLESS

Pollock's parents tried and failed at farming and various other jobs and were always moving. By the time Pollock was eight, his father worked away from home and sent the family a cheque each month. Pollock found it hard to make friends and felt like an outsider. When he was 15, he began drinking and was expelled from his school's Reserve Officers' Training Corps for fighting.

As a boy, Pollock did not show any talent as an artist. His eldest brother, Charles, seemed more

▲ Sande, Jackson and Jay (front) with their father on a visit to the Grand Canyon in the summer of 1927.

talented. In 1922, Charles enrolled at the Otis Art Institute in Los Angeles. The arts magazines he sent home introduced Pollock and Sande (the fourth brother) to modern European art and inspired them with artistic ambitions. In 1928, Pollock enrolled at Manual Arts High School, Los Angeles.

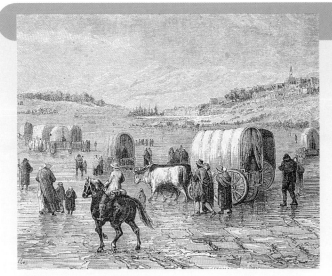

▲ The trek west. Pollock's grandparents had come to America from the British Isles in the 19th century, looking for a better life.

HEADING WEST

During the 1800s, millions of people moved to the United States. They came from all over Europe and Asia. Most were escaping poverty or persecution in their native lands. All were attracted by the promise of fortunes to be made, usually by farming or prospecting in the West.

The reality was rather different. Not all the immigrants survived the journey to America. Those who arrived safely often ran out of money before they could stake a claim to any land. Instead, they worked in towns or on the railways. Those who did settle in the West led hard lives. Many died of starvation or disease. The Native Americans were often unfriendly, as were white Americans already settled in the West.

When Pollock's parents moved to Cody, there was still free land to be claimed – but settlers needed money to build on it. The Pollocks did not have money to buy timber and so had to rent a home instead.

Becoming an artist

When he was at Manual Arts, Pollock tried to dress and behave like an artist, and he soaked up new ideas. His art tutor introduced him to theosophy, a branch of Hindu mysticism that had been developed by a Russian spiritualist called Helena Blavatsky in the 1870s. The teachings of theosophy made sense to the young artist, but Pollock's brother Charles was less impressed. In letters he told Pollock that theosophy was escapism. He recommended that Pollock look for meaning in the pictures of the Mexican muralists instead (see panel).

Pollock knew he wanted to be an artist, but not what sort. His drawing frustrated him and he admitted to Charles: 'my drawing I will tell you frankly is rotten, it seems to lack freedom and rhythm, it is cold and lifeless…' At this time he seemed more likely to turn to sculpture than painting.

'As to what I would like to be. An artist of some kind.'

Pollock writing to his brother, Charles

◀ *Untitled (Self-Portrait)*, c.1931-35. This dark and shadowy self-portrait is Pollock's earliest surviving work.

TIMELINE ▶

June 1930	September 1930	Autumn 1931
Pollock and Charles see Orozco's *Prometheus* mural.	Pollock moves to New York. Enrols at the Art Students League.	Pollock enrols for Thomas Hart Benton's mural class.

▲ This portrait of Pollock was taken in New York in 1931, while he was a pupil at the Art Students League.

TROUBLE-MAKERS

Pollock's closest friends at art school were Philip Goldstein (1913-80; later to become Philip Guston, another Abstract Expressionist) and Manuel Tolegian (1911-83). Together, the three men published and distributed a student newsletter, *The Journal of Liberty*. In his second term Pollock was expelled. He returned a year later, but was thrown out again, this time for fighting with a teacher.

Pollock headed to New York and enrolled at the Art Students League, where Charles had been since 1926. He signed up for mural classes with Thomas Hart Benton (1889-1975). Benton hated abstract art, but he taught his pupils to look for the underlying patterns in a picture. Pollock began to learn the basics of composition at last.

MEXICO'S MURALISTS

The Mexican mural movement was at its peak in the early 1930s. The muralists believed that art could help change society for the better. They were encouraged by President Obregón of Mexico who commissioned public art, especially murals, that celebrated Mexico's rich, Aztec past. Three leading Mexican muralists, Diego Rivera (1886-1957), José Clemente Orozco (1883-1949) and David Alfaro Siqueiros (1896-1974), all spent time in the US.

In June 1930, Pollock and Charles saw Orozco's *Prometheus* fresco in Claremont, California. It was raw, violent and energetic – and paid little attention to conventions such as scale. The brothers saw Orozco working at the New School for Social Research in New York that winter. He was painting a mural series two floors up from Thomas Hart Benton, their tutor at the Art Students League.

Rivera was the most famous of the three Mexican artists. In 1933, Pollock watched him paint his *Man at the Crossroads* mural in New York's Rockefeller Center. This work was destroyed before it was finished because it featured Vladimir Lenin, the Communist leader of the Russian Revolution. Siqueiros was the most outspoken and politically active of the Mexican muralists. In 1936, Pollock would work directly for Siqueiros in his workshop.

▲ Diego Rivera at work on the Rockefeller Center mural in 1933.

Teacher's pet

◄ Thomas Hart Benton was Pollock's most influential tutor at the Art Students League in New York.

THE GREAT DEPRESSION

In October 1929 US share prices suddenly fell, making many people's savings worthless overnight. Families and companies were ruined and the economic crisis spread to other countries. Before long, nearly half the banks in America were bankrupt and more than a quarter of the population had lost their jobs.

In 1932 Franklin Roosevelt became President. He launched a New Deal policy which aimed to help the poorest people in society, and to boost the economy by funding new projects such as buildings and public works of art.

This created some jobs, but the Depression did not truly end until 1939. Then World War II broke out and many workers were needed by factories producing parachutes, bombs and jeeps.

Pollock's art teacher, Thomas Hart Benton, was a Regionalist painter. When painting, he applied oil paints thickly and swiftly for impact. He wanted to record a perfect image of America's recent past – cowboys, wagon trains, saloons, mine shafts and dramatic landscapes. These subjects were very popular, partly because so many people were struggling to make a living at the time (see panel).

Other Regionalist painters were Grant Wood (1892-1942) and John Steuart Curry (1897-1946).

Pollock admired Benton's work and experimented with similar subjects in his pictures *Camp with Oil Rig* and *Going West*. Pollock almost captured the older painter's style, but his works were far gloomier.

A SECOND FAMILY

Benton made Pollock his class monitor and the struggling young artist was one of his favourites outside school, too. Pollock ate with the Bentons at least once a week and, from 1934 until 1937, he often stayed at their holiday home on Martha's Vineyard, an island off the coast of Massachusetts.

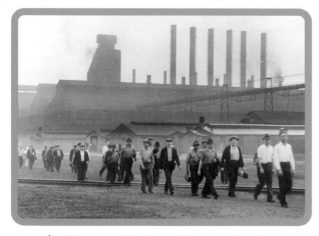

▲ Chicago steelworkers. Jobs were hard to come by in the mid-1930s.

TIMELINE ▶

1932	1933	Spring 1934	Winter 1934
Benton goes on sabbatical so he can paint a mural for the Chicago World Fair.	Pollock sees Rivera paint Rockefeller Center mural.	Pollock first visits the Bentons on Martha's Vineyard.	Sande moves in with Pollock. The brothers share a school cleaning job.

Going West c.1934-38

oil on gesso on fibreboard 38.3 x 52.7 cm National Museum of American Art, Smithsonian Institution, Washington DC

**A ghostly figure drives the team of mules westward. The wagons and the empty, mountainous landscape
are all-American subject matter and show the influence of Pollock's teacher, Benton. Pollock borrowed the
glowing moon and whirling, urgent brushstrokes from one of his tutor's seascapes.**

*'Pollock was a born artist. The only thing I taught
him was how to drink a fifth [of whisky] a day.'*

Thomas Hart Benton

On and off the Project

▲ A 1935 FAP exhibition poster.

In spring 1936 Pollock and his brother Sande volunteered to help in David Alfaro Siqueiros' workshop, which was producing Communist posters and floats for the New York May Day Parade. The politics did not interest Pollock, but the Mexican's methods did. Siqueiros experimented with blowtorches and spray guns, used industrial materials such as cement and car paints – and even splattered paint.

Pollock tried out these techniques in his own studio, but he was finding it difficult to paint at all. He had joined the Federal Art Project in 1935 (see panel) but some of his works for them were rejected. Depressed, Pollock turned to drink. He missed deadlines and the FAP fired him.

SEEKING HELP

From June 1938 Pollock spent four months at Bloomingdale Asylum, trying to solve his drinking problem. Doctors there used art therapy to help their patients and Pollock made some beautiful copper plates and bowls. Once he was out of hospital, he started drinking again, but he was also painting again and the FAP took him back. Pollock's new works, such as *Untitled (Naked Man with Knife)*, owed a lot to the violent José Orozco murals he admired.

PAID TO PAINT

From 1935 to 1942 Pollock worked for the Federal Art Project, set up as part of the New Deal. At its peak, the FAP employed about 5,000 artists, including Arshile Gorky (1904-48), Willem de Kooning (1904-97), Philip Guston and Mark Rothko (1903-70). Pollock was paid $23.50 a week for creating a painting a month – although he did not always manage this.

The artworks were for schools, post offices and other public buildings, but many went into storage and were later destroyed.

◀ The Mexican artist Siqueiros (left) with Pollock (right) at the May Day Parade in New York, 1936.

TIMELINE ▶

1935	1936	1937	1938
Pollock joins the Federal Art Project (FAP), which later becomes the WPA Art Program. He is employed by the Program until it closes in 1942.	Pollock sees two important exhibitions: 'Cubism and Abstract Art' and 'Fantastic Art, Dada, Surrealism'. He joins Siqueiros' experimental May Day workshop and sees Orozco's *The Epic of American Civilization*.	Pollock tries Jungian therapy for the first time.	Pollock is treated at Bloomingdale Asylum. He moves to the FAP easel division.

Untitled (Naked Man with Knife), c.1938-40

oil on canvas 127 x 91.4 cm Tate Gallery, London

Pollock talked about the late 1930s as a time of 'violent changes' in his art. This painting
of a ritual killing shows his struggle. Pollock's earlier works had included small figures or
none at all, but this one has two massive, muscular figures. The one on the right is about
to plunge a knife into the other. Pollock captures this plunging action with a freeze-frame
effect, showing the movement of the knife and the turn of the killer's head.

Meeting of minds

JUNGIAN THERAPY

Pollock began seeing Dr Joseph Henderson for therapy in 1939. Henderson was a follower of Carl Jung (1875-1961), the Swiss psychotherapist who said that there is a 'collective unconscious' buried deep in everyone's mind, as deep and as important as the foundations of a house. Jung believed that the unconscious is a treasure-chest of stories and pictures that feed our imaginations.

Pollock was too shy to talk about his dreams and feelings. Instead, he took Henderson his drawings to analyse. According to Jung, art could reveal clues to psychological problems, because both tap the unconscious mind.

▲ Swiss psychotherapist Carl Jung.

▲ *Abstract Human Figure* painted by Lee Krasner in 1938.

In 1937 Pollock met John Graham. Graham was a painter, critic and curator, who had moved to New York in 1917 to escape the Russian Revolution. He loved primitive art and especially the art of Pablo Picasso (1881-1973). Graham saw great promise in Pollock. He admired *Birth* with its flattened perspective and mask motifs, and included it in the exhibition 'American and French Paintings' which he organised in 1942. This showed works by big-name European artists, such as Pablo Picasso, Henri Matisse (1869-1954) and Georges Braque (1882-1963), hanging alongside unknown Americans such as Willem de Kooning, Lee Krasner (1908-84) and Pollock himself.

LOVE AT FIRST SIGHT

Lenore (or Lee) Krasner was a Brooklyn-born Jewish painter. She had studied under the avant-garde artist Hans Hofmann (1880-1966) and had begun to make her own abstract still-lifes. When Krasner learned that Pollock's work was included in the 1942 show alongside hers, she was intrigued and sought him out. She said of Pollock: 'I fell in love with him – physically, mentally – in every sense of the word.' The pair discovered that they shared a love of Picasso and an interest in Jung (see panel). Krasner recognised Pollock's genius at once. 'I had a conviction when I met Jackson that he had something important to say,' she said.

TIMELINE ▶

1939	1940	1941	1942
Pollock starts therapy with Dr Joseph Henderson. He sees Picasso's *Guernica* and a Picasso retrospective at MoMA. The FAP becomes the WPA Art Program.	Dr Henderson refers Pollock to Dr Violet Staub de Laszlo.	Pollock sees the 'Indian Art of the United States' exhibition. The World War II draft board says he is not fit enough to fight. Peggy Guggenheim arrives in New York.	John Graham includes *Birth* in 'American and French Paintings'. Pollock and Krasner become lovers. Art of This Century gallery opens.

Birth c.1941

oil on canvas 116.4 x 55.1 cm
Tate Gallery, London

For Pollock, painting was a creative act, just like giving birth. Instead of a baby, the end result was a work of art – in this case, thick with colourful oil paints. Among the swirling shapes you can make out emblems that look like Native American masks, including an eagle with a beady eye and a pale pink beak just off-centre.

'I'm in a bog. I can't do anything.'

Jackson Pollock, talking about the problems he experienced with his painting

Big names from Paris

At the start of the 20th century Paris was the undisputed capital of the art world. Key French art movements of the time included Symbolism, as seen in the works of Paul Gauguin (1848-1903), Pierre Bonnard (1867-1947) and Henri Rousseau (1844-1910); and Fauvism, as practised by Henri Matisse and André Derain (1880-1954). But the most influential movements, especially as far as Pollock was concerned, were Cubism, led by Pablo Picasso and Georges Braque, and Surrealism, whose most famous artist is Salvador Dalí (1904-89).

France's position changed when World War II began in 1939. France was defeated by Nazi Germany in

▲ Facing the threat of Nazi invasion, many Europeans crossed the Atlantic to seek safety in the United States.

June 1940. The German army occupied about three-fifths of the country, and the rest was governed by French collaborators. France was not freed from Nazi control until September 1944.

A SAFE HAVEN

During the war many artists and collectors fled to New York. They included Roberto Matta (1911-2002), Salvador Dalí, Fernand Léger (1881-1955), Piet Mondrian (1872-1944), André Masson (1896-1987) and André Breton (1896-1966).

Breton had founded the Surrealist movement. He was not a painter but a poet. He wrote manifestos which spelled out the aims of the Surrealists.

◀ *Composition No. 8*, c. 1942, Piet Mondrian. The Dutch abstract artist Mondrian moved from Paris to London in 1938, and then to New York in 1940. Mondrian is best known for his straight-line grids and squares of primary colours.

Breton's first manifesto introduced the idea of 'automatism': relaxing and switching off so that you can write or paint from your unconscious (the hidden part of the mind where deepest desires are stored).

In New York, the artist Roberto Matta set up a Saturday afternoon group to discuss and explore Surrealist techniques. Pollock went to these meetings but was too shy to say much. To some, he seemed stand-offish. The sculptor David Hare (1917-91) said: 'Jackson didn't like the Surrealists because he thought they were anti-American. And the Surrealists didn't like him because... Jackson wouldn't court them at all.'

▲ Art collector Peggy Guggenheim with her dogs. She inherited her vast fortune in 1912 after her father died when the *Titanic* sank.

ART'S FIRST LADY

The return of American heiress Peggy Guggenheim (1898-1979) to New York in 1941 changed Pollock's fortunes. Guggenheim had moved to Europe after World War I. She lived in London and Paris, where she collected and dealt in modern art. Her name was linked with the Surrealists, and she was briefly married to one, Max Ernst (1891-1976). On her return to New York Guggenheim opened her Art of This Century gallery in 1942. There she 'discovered' and promoted the New York School (the Abstract Expressionists). After the war, in 1947, Guggenheim returned to live in Europe.

◀ New York's Guggenheim Museum was built to house the art collection of Peggy's uncle, Solomon R. Guggenh... The museum was designed by Fr... Lloyd Wright and opened in 19...

Confusing canvases

By autumn 1942, Lee Krasner had moved into Pollock's apartment on East 8th Street in New York. She introduced him to her friends, who included the Surrealist Roberto Matta, the critic Clement Greenberg (1909-94) and the painter Hans Hofmann. Her admiration boosted Pollock's confidence. In a burst of creativity, he made three large, energetic paintings, including *Stenographic Figure* (see opposite).

ART IN SHORTHAND

Matta introduced Pollock to Peggy Guggenheim in 1943 and she asked him to submit a piece for her first Spring Salon at her Art of This Century gallery. Pollock sent in *Stenographic Figure* (originally called *Painting*). One of the judges was Piet Mondrian, the famous Dutch abstract artist. 'I have a feeling this may be the most exciting painting that I have seen in a long, long time, here or in Europe,' he said.

▲ *Harlequin's Carnival*, Joan Miró, 1924-25. The colourful shapes look like strange dancing insects.

Stenographic Figure has yellow, black and white graffiti-like squiggles, and is clearly influenced by the work of Joan Miró (1893-1983, see panel). Pollock was interested in how the Surrealists expressed on canvas their fleeting thoughts and deep desires.

▲ Joan Miró found international fame in the early 1940s with a solo show at the Museum of Modern Art (MoMA) in New York.

MIRO AND THE SURREALISTS

Pollock probably first saw Joan Miró's work at the Museum of Modern Art's exhibition 'Fantastic Art, Dada, Surrealism', which ran from December 1936 to January 1937.

The Spanish artist is famous for his bold, colourful symbols set against heavily-painted backgrounds. It's as if the symbols are Miró's unconscious thoughts and fantasies swimming to the surface.

In 1941 MoMA put on a huge Miró retrospective, which Pollock also saw.

TIMELINE ▶

Autumn 1942	January 1943	April 1943	May 1943
Krasner moves into Pollock's apartment.	Pollock shows *The Flame* at the Metropolitan Museum of Art's 'Artists for Victory'.	*Collage* (now lost) is included in Art of This Century's international collage show.	Pollock submits *Stenographic Figure* for Guggenheim's 'Spring Salon for Young Artists'.

Stenographic Figure, c.1942

oil on linen 101.6 x 142.2 cm The Museum of Modern Art, New York

A stenographer is a shorthand typist. Some people looking at this painting can see a woman sitting typing, her arms crossing as her hands whizz over the keys. Most people, however, see the outline of a reclining nude. Pollock never attached much importance to titles, but perhaps this one is helpful. Could it refer to the sketchy quality of the figure – as though it has been drawn in shorthand?

'You must watch this man.'

Mondrian talking about Pollock after seeing Stenographic Figure

All-American

▲ Navajo Indians make a sand painting. First, the design is scratched in the sand with a stick. Then the coloured pigments are sprinkled into the grooves.

AMERICAN ORIGINALS

Pollock went to the Museum of Modern Art's 1941 exhibition, 'Indian Art of the United States', more than once.

He also attended a linked event at which Navajo Indians made sand paintings on the floor. The Navajo considered the ritual of making a painting more sacred than the finished picture. A sand painting could only be temporary, after all, because the sand would soon blow away.

M ondrian was not the only friend of Guggenheim's to be impressed by *Stenographic Figure*. French-born Marcel Duchamp (1887-1968) was another. The enthusiasm of the two artists convinced Guggenheim to give Pollock his first one-man show. She also commissioned a Pollock mural for her own apartment. Howard Putzel, her gallery assistant, even persuaded her to give Pollock a fixed monthly salary. Pollock gave up his job as a lift attendant and devoted himself to painting full-time.

BACK TO BASICS

Excited about his first solo show, Pollock painted with tremendous energy. More than ever, he drew inspiration from primitive art, especially that of Native Americans. Pollock had come across Native American culture as a boy, when he had seen reservation Indians selling hand-made blankets, and had also explored village ruins in the West.

◄ Pollock and Guggenheim stand before the huge mural he painted for her apartment hall. Pollock had agonized over the commission for months, then completed it in a single night of frenzied work.

TIMELINE ▶

1943	May 1943	November 1943
Guggenheim commissions a mural from Pollock for her apartment.	Guggenheim gives Pollock a monthly salary. He gives up his job as a lift attendant.	Pollock's first solo show opens at Art of This Century.

The Moon-Woman Cuts the Circle, c.1943

oil on canvas 109.5 x 104 cm Musée national d'art moderne, Centre de Création Industrielle,
Centre Georges Pompidou, Paris

In a riot of blue, red and yellow, Pollock dances a victorious war dance! More than any
other, this painting shows the artist's delight in borrowing from Native American art.
The painting even includes a figure in a feathered headdress.

'Pollock's talent is volcanic... It is lavish, explosive, untidy...'

The critic James Johnson Sweeney, in the exhibition catalogue for Pollock's first solo show

A noticeable influence

PICASSO'S *GUERNICA*

Pollock first saw Pablo Picasso's *Guernica* (1937) in May 1939.

Guernica, a city in northern Spain, was heavily bombed during the Spanish Civil War (1936-39). Picasso wanted to draw attention to the brutality of the bombing. He believed that art could be used as a weapon against such horrors.

Picasso emphasises the horror by distorting the figures. The victims become absolute essences or archetypes. The weeping woman is a good example. She appears on the left-hand side of the painting, clutching her dead child.

The painting was exhibited to raise money for refugees from the Spanish Civil War.

Reviewers of Pollock's first solo exhibition were quick to recognise in his paintings the influence of Pablo Picasso. In 1939, at a time when Pollock was struggling to find a new direction with his painting, Picasso's work was on show in several places in New York. Picasso's influence is most clear in the powerful centrepiece of Pollock's first exhibition, *The She-Wolf* (see right).

'The effect of his one noticeable influence, Picasso, is a healthy one, for it imposes a certain symmetry on his work without detracting from its basic force and vigour.'

Robert Coates in a review of Pollock's first show

SPLIT PERSONALITY

The creature in the painting has two heads, but neither is that of a wolf. On the left is a bull's head, similar to Picasso's stylised bulls. But the head on the right is all-American. It's a buffalo, just like the one on dime (10-cent) coins. Pollock refused to explain *The She-Wolf*, saying that it 'came into existence because I had to paint it. Any attempt on my part to say something about it… could only destroy it.'

▲ *Guernica*, Pablo Picasso, 1937. The painting was exhibited in New York's Valentine Gallery during May 1939. Pollock went to see it many times and made several sketches of it.

The She-Wolf, c.1943

oil, gouache and plaster on canvas 106.4 x 170.2 cm The Museum of Modern Art, New York

At the time he painted *The She-Wolf*, Pollock was beginning to loosen up and become much more abstract.
Beneath the solid grey edging the surface of the canvas was originally covered in multi-coloured splatters.
On the left-hand side, a drip of grey has trickled down over the beast's neck. *The She-Wolf* was the first Pollock
painting to be bought by a museum – it was bought by the Museum of Modern Art in April 1944 for $400.

'I had to paint it.'

Pollock, talking about The She-Wolf

The war years

▲ A mushroom cloud fills the sky above Nagasaki, Japan, after the US dropped an atom bomb there on 9 August 1945.

THE HORROR OF WAR

When World War II started in 1939 the United States did not become actively involved.

But, on 7 December 1941, the Japanese made a surprise attack on Pearl Harbor, a US base on Hawaii, and the US declared war on Japan and Germany.

In August 1945 the US forced Japan's surrender after dropping atom bombs on the cities of Hiroshima and Nagasaki. The bombs killed more than 100,000 people outright and, through radiation poisoning, many more in the years after.

While Pollock was making a name for himself as an artist, America was at war (1941-45).

The closest Pollock came to helping the war effort was through what had been the Federal Art Project. Following a letter his therapist wrote to the draft board, Pollock had been classified as unfit to fight in 1941. From June to December 1942, Krasner employed him on her poster-making team as part of the new WPA Art Program's War Services Department. Then the program was disbanded.

SKETCHED ATROCITIES

The violence in the paintings Pollock produced during the war mainly reflects his own psychological problems, not the wartime horrors happening in the world. But his sketchbooks are different. Here, Pollock was working in coloured inks, pencils and gouache – faster media than slow-drying oils – and was able to show his immediate reaction to events.

▲ Ships ablaze in Pearl Harbor, December 1941. Japanese bomber, fighter and torpedo planes devastated the US fleet, and shocked the American nation.

TIMELINE ▶

1944	Spring 1945	1945
Pollock paints *Mural* for Peggy Guggenheim's town house. It is too wide, so Pollock trims it! MoMA buys *The She-Wolf* – the first museum to buy a Pollock painting.	Pollock's second solo show at Art of This Century. A Pollock exhibition opens at The Arts Club of Chicago; it will later be shown at the San Francisco Museum of Art.	Guggenheim renews her contract with Pollock, doubling his monthly income to $300. In return, she receives all the paintings of the next year except one.

War, c.1944-46 (dated 1947)

ink and colour pencil on paper 52.4 x 66 cm The Metropolitan Museum of Art, New York

In this sketch, *War*, Pollock drew terrifying tangles of people, bonfire piles of war dead and figures riddled with bullet holes. He also used ink to add splatters, smears and pourings of blood.

Change of scene

◀ Krasner and Pollock at Springs in 1946. That summer Pollock started using the barn as his studio, while Krasner used an upstairs bedroom as hers.

Pollock and Krasner married in October 1945 and moved to Long Island. Today, Springs is fashionable and expensive, but then it was a cheap, quiet backwater. Their farmhouse, set in two hectares, cost $5,000. 'We wanted to get away from the wear and tear,' said Pollock. 'Besides, I had an underneath confidence that I could begin to live on my painting.'

The house had no heating, electricity or plumbing and the first winter was extremely hard. Working in a cramped upstairs bedroom Pollock produced *Yellow Triangle*, *The Tea Cup*, *The Water Bull* and *The Key*. He named these colourful, abstract oil paintings the 'Accabonac Creek' series, after the little stream that ran past the house. Already, Pollock had almost stopped using an easel (*The Key*, for example, has floorboard marks on the back).

Pollock's next series, 'Sounds in the Grass', was more abstract still. In *Shimmering Substance* and *Eyes in the Heat*, Pollock created his first 'allover' paintings.

ALLOVER PAINTINGS

Pollock's 'allovers' were dense chaotic repetitions all over the canvas – in *Eyes in the Heat*, for example, he showed teeming eyes. The effect was to dissolve the painting into what Clement Greenberg called 'sheer sensation'. Terms like 'top' and 'bottom' were meaningless, and no one part of the canvas was more important than any other.

▲ Part of the floor in Pollock's studio in Springs, covered with marks left by the allover paintings.

TIMELINE ▶

25 October 1945	1946	April 1946	December 1946
Pollock marries Lee Krasner at the Marble Collegiate Church on Fifth Avenue. A week later they move to Springs, East Hampton, on Long Island.	Pollock works on his 'Accabonac Creek' and 'Sounds in the Grass' series, moving into his studio barn that summer. He designs the cover for Guggenheim's memoir, *Out of This Century*.	Pollock's third solo show for Guggenheim opens in April and includes *Troubled Queen*.	Pollock is included in the *Whitney Annual* for the first time, with *Two*.

The Key (Accabonac Creek series), 1946

oil on canvas 149.8 x 213.3 cm The Art Institute of Chicago

Pollock moved his studio barn from the back yard to the side of the house so that the house would no longer block his view of the creek. The Long Island landscape inspired him to paint a series of colourful, optimistic abstracts.

'Such winds. It's all very nice, tho' a little tuff on a city slicker.'

Pollock, writing to Ed Strautlin, his former neighbour in New York

Breakthrough

▲ Pollock (on the left) with British artist Peter Blake at the Betty Parsons Gallery in 1949.

THE BETTY PARSONS GALLERY

In May 1947 Guggenheim moved back to Europe and Betty Parsons (1900-82) took over some of her artists. Parsons was an art dealer who had lived in Paris during the 1920s and returned to America in 1933. She opened her first gallery in 1946.

Because of Pollock's drinking Guggenheim had difficulty finding someone to take over her contract when she returned to Europe. Parsons later said that 'Pollock was dumped in my lap because no-one else would risk showing him.' None of the artists that Parsons took over from Guggenheim had yet found fame. By 1950, the Parsons Gallery had shown not only Pollock's drip paintings, but also the mature styles of Clyfford Still (1904-80), Mark Rothko (1903-70) and Barnett Newman (1905-70).

During 1947 Pollock worked towards his first show for the Betty Parsons Gallery on East 57th Street. He wrote to a friend, 'I'm just now getting into painting again and the stuff is really beginning to flow. Grand feeling when it happens.'

Pollock had made an amazing breakthrough. With new works such as *Galaxy*, *Cathedral* and *Full Fathom Five*, he had found his 'drip' technique. As Willem de Kooning grudgingly put it, Pollock 'busted our idea of a picture all to hell'. But not everyone agreed this was a good thing.

CRITICS ON THE FENCE

Response to the Betty Parsons' show was lukewarm and just one painting was bought. Reviewers saw energy in the work, but did not understand it. 'It will be interesting to see the reactions,' wrote a reviewer in the magazine *Art Digest*.

◄ Dutch-born Willem de Kooning had settled in New York in 1927. He was one of the best-known leaders of the New York School.

When *Life* magazine ran an article on 'Young American Extremists' later that year, *Cathedral* was among the paintings featured. *Cathedral* was 'a pleasant design for a necktie,' said a Yale professor. Pollock's work appeared too decorative to be serious.

TIMELINE ▶

January 1947	April/May 1947	1948
Pollock's fourth solo show opens at Art of This Century. It includes *Mural* and the *Accabonac Creek* and the *Sounds in the Grass* series.	Pollock exhibits *Mural* in the 'Large Scale Modern Paintings' exhibition at MoMA. Art of This Century closes. Betty Parsons takes on Pollock.	Pollock's Betty Parsons show includes *Alchemy*, *Cathedral*, *Comet* and *Full Fathom Five*. Guggenheim shows *Eyes in the Heat*, *The Moon Woman* and *Two* at the XXIV Venice Biennale.

Full Fathom Five, 1947

oil on canvas with nails,
tacks, buttons, key, coins,
cigarettes, matches, etc.
129.2 x 76.5 cm
The Museum of Modern Art,
New York

**The deeply crusted surface
contains artefacts from the
real world – drawing pins
and buttons, paint-tube
caps and cigarette ends.
The painting was built up,
layer after layer, to create
the rich sea-green swell.
The black-encircled orange
and yellow anchor shape
was the last element to
be added.**

Jack the Dripper

Pollock is best known for the dynamic drip paintings which he produced between 1947 and 1951. Instead of standing at an easel, Pollock placed canvases on the floor. He said, 'I feel nearer, more a part of the painting since this way I can walk around it, work from the four sides and literally be in the painting, similar to the Indian sand painters of the West...'

Flinging the paint at the canvas, spattering on drips from the end of a stick – Pollock was using his whole body. And Pollock denied that the works were the product of chance. Even if it was unconsciously, his own rhythms drove or created the painting. 'When I am in my painting, I'm not aware of what I'm doing,' said Pollock. 'It is only after a sort of "get acquainted" period that I see what I have been about... The painting has a life of its own. I try to let it come through. It is only

▲ An overall view of the floor of Pollock's studio (see also the close-up on page 26). It almost looks like a drip painting!

when I lose contact with the painting that the result is a mess. Otherwise there is pure harmony, an easy give and take, and the painting comes out well.'

ACTION PAINTING

The critic Harold Rosenberg coined the term action painting to describe Pollock's way of painting. In his 1952 *Art News* article 'The American Action Painters', he said that for some artists the canvas had become 'an arena in which to act', rather than somewhere simply to show a picture. Rosenberg believed that the act of painting was more important than the finished work.

Pollock was not happy with Rosenberg's action-painting article. For him, the point was simply to find the truest expression of himself. And since he only really felt alive when he was painting

◀ The house in Springs where Pollock's drip paintings were done. This photo was taken in May 1992.

▲ One of the several thousand photographs taken by Hans Namuth showing Pollock at work.

and creating, his art had to be about painting. As the artist Helen Frankenthaler said, it was no use talking to Pollock 'about life or art. One experienced the man quiet or the man wild. I guess he was his true self when painting. That's where he lived.'

CAUGHT ON CAMERA

During the summer of 1950 the photographer Hans Namuth documented Pollock's technique. Image after image shows Pollock prowling around the edge of his canvas, pouring, flicking and flinging paint. He used sticks, trowels and hardened brushes to apply the paint, or sometimes his own hands.

Namuth said: 'It was a great drama – the flame of explosion when the paint hit the canvas; the dance-like movement; the eyes tormented before knowing where to strike… my hands were trembling.'

'Energy and motion made visible – memories arrested in space.'

Pollock, explaining his drip paintings

The height of fame

Pollock's second show for Betty Parsons, which opened in January 1949, was reviewed everywhere, thanks to an article published in *Life* magazine the previous autumn. The article had featured comments from leading figures on modern paintings, including Pollock's *Cathedral*. Art critic Clement Greenberg was enthusiastic, saying that *Number 1A, 1948* (see right) was like a Renaissance masterpiece. Even *Time* magazine printed one of the paintings. Most write-ups were mocking, but that did not matter. Pollock's work was selling.

SUGAR DADDY

One buyer was Alfonso Ossorio, an artist and collector from a family of sugar growers. Over the next few years, Ossorio would buy more than a dozen Pollocks. He bought a country estate in East Hampton and also offered the Pollocks free use of his New York house. Pollock had a wealthy patron at last.

▲ Pollock's fifth solo show at the Betty Parsons Gallery included watercolours, drawings and 21 new oil paintings.

INTERNATIONAL STARDOM

Recognition in Europe was just around the corner. *Number 1A, 1948* was one of three Pollock paintings shown at the 1950 Venice Biennale. To coincide with the Biennale, Peggy Guggenheim gave Pollock a solo show in the city. Reviewing this, Italian critic Bruno Alfieri called Pollock's work chaotic, but also said it made Picasso look like 'a painter of the past'. Pollock was delighted!

◀ Pollock and Krasner photographed in Pollock's studio, 1949.

WHAT'S IN A NAME?

From 1948 onwards, Pollock stopped naming his paintings and instead referred to them by number and year. (Betty Parsons later added an 'A' after some of the numbers to indicate paintings that had previously been seen, but were still unsold.)

Pollock said the numbers stopped 'adding to the confusion'. They were neutral, whereas names suggested meanings. Even so, many of the paintings came to have popular names. For example, the painting that Pollock officially called *Number 1, 1950* is much better known as *Lavender Mist*.

TIMELINE ▶

Autumn 1948	January 1949	August 1949	Autumn 1949	November 1949
Pollock begins treatment for alcoholism with Dr Edwin Heller.	At Pollock's second show for Betty Parsons, all the paintings have 'neutral' numbers, not names.	*Life* magazine prints 'Jackson Pollock: Is he the greatest living painter in the United States?'	Two Pollock sculptures shown in MoMA's 'Sculpture by Painters'. Pollock also exhibits in 'The Intrasubjectives' at the Kootz Gallery.	Pollock's third show at Betty Parsons opens.

Number 1A, 1948

oil und enamel on canvas 172.7 x 264.2 cm The Museum of Modern Art, New York

Pollock stopped composing his pictures in a way that gave more importance to certain elements than to others. The drip paintings are intended to be seen in their entirety, all at once. Pollock uses handprints (top right) to add to the sense of urgency, so that the creation of the work is immediate, with no space between him and the canvas. But though the handprints look spontaneous, Pollock actually touched up the right-hand ones. He filled in the missing fingertip that he'd lost as a young boy while playing at chopping wood.

'The stuff is really beginning to flow...'

Jackson Pollock

The Abstract Expressionists

Pollock was not the only American artist making waves at the end of the 1940s. Many of his contemporaries shared his aim of expressing powerful, deep-felt emotions through abstract art – and like him, they did so on huge, larger-than-life canvases. As early as 1945 this art movement of (mostly New York-based) painters was named Abstract Expressionism.

The Abstract Expressionists may have been grouped together, but they had very individual styles of painting. Those most similar to Pollock were Willem de Kooning, Franz Kline (1910-62), Lee Krasner and Robert Motherwell (1915-91). Like him, they stressed the act of painting. Instead of flinging or dripping paint, they used urgent, energetic brushstrokes.

FIELDS OF COLOUR

Another branch of Abstract Expressionism was colour-field painting, the use of large areas of more or less flat colour. For example, Barnett Newman painted in a single colour and then add one or two contrasting 'zips' (vertical stripes). Ad Reinhardt (1913-67), tried out monochrome (single-colour) canvases, often blue or red.

Russian-born Mark Rothko created large, messy-edged rectangles of colour that seemed to float in front of the painting. Rothko explained the aim of his art: to express 'basic human emotions – tragedy, ecstasy, doom and so on… The people who weep before my pictures are having the same religious experience I had when I painted them.'

▲ *Eve*, Barnett Newman, 1950. Newman used massive canvases: *Eve* is 2.4 metres high and 1.7 metres wide and almost completely taken up with a huge expanse of red. Only a single vertical dark streak – one of Newman's 'zips' – breaks the flow.

TIMELINE ▶

December 1949	January 1950	May 1950	Summer 1950	October 1950
Number 14, 1949 on exhibition at the Whitney Museum of American Art.	MoMA buys *Number 1A, 1948*. Pollock and Krasner winter with Ossorio in New York.	Pollock boycotts the Metropolitan Museum of Art's painting exhibition.	Three Pollock paintings represent the US at the XXV Venice Biennale; Pollock has a solo show in Venice, too. Hans Namuth photographs Pollock at work.	Pollock's *Number 8, 1950* is included in Leo Castelli's 'Young Painters in the US & France' exhibition.

> *'I'm not an abstract artist...*
> *I'm interested only in*
> *expressing basic human*
> *emotions.'*
>
> Mark Rothko

WORKING TOGETHER

Pollock was too insecure and too much of a loner to socialise much with his fellow artists. And many of them, in turn, either resented Pollock's success or disliked his rudeness. Even so, Pollock was involved in a couple of group events.

The first was a demonstration in front of MoMA (the Museum of Modern Art, New York) in May 1949. The demonstrators were angry about the Institute of Modern Art in Boston changing its name to the Institute of Contemporary Art. As the *New York Times* pointed out, this was so the museum could

▲ *Untitled*, Mark Rothko, c.1951-52. Rothko wanted the viewer to be swallowed up in his colourful trademark rectangles. Here, they are painted using different layers of orange, yellow, green, blue and white.

keep out 'experimental meanderings' by artists such as Pollock.

A year later, Pollock was one of a group of 18 painters and 10 sculptors who decided to boycott the Metropolitan Museum of Art. They said there was no point in entering the museum's annual art competition because it was prejudiced against 'advanced art'.

The protesters became known as the 'Irascibles' (Angry Ones); in January 1951 *Life* magazine printed a picture of the serious-looking group.

◀ The artist Mark Rothko. Tragically, he committed suicide in 1970.

Drink and depression

On 25 November 1950, after Hans Namuth had finished filming him, Pollock had his first drink for two years. Perhaps posing had made him feel a fake. Or maybe Pollock missed the support of his doctor, who had died six months earlier. Maybe he was worried about his next show.

Even after the show was a huge success, Pollock could not overcome his self-doubt and he spent the rest of his life trying to escape through drink. 'He thought he was the greatest painter ever, but at the same time he wondered,' said Betty Parsons.

▲ Pollock and Krasner at a family reunion in the summer of 1950. Pollock's mother, Stella, is in the centre of the photograph.

PAINT IT BLACK

In 1951-52 Pollock did a series of paintings in which he dribbled and poured black enamel over the canvas. He wrote: 'I've had a period of drawing on canvas in black – with some of my early images coming thru – think the non-objectivists will find them disturbing – and the kids who think it simple to splash a Pollock out.' Against the raw, cream canvas the effect of the black enamel is melancholy and graphic, a complete contrast to the energy and colour of Pollock's previous work.

Pollock completed a few more drip paintings, but really he had finished using that technique.

CEDAR STREET TAVERN

One of New York's most popular artists' bars was Cedar Street Tavern in Greenwich Village. It was packed and noisy. Big-name artists such as Kline, Guston and de Kooning went there to hold court before a gaggle of art students.

But admirers of Pollock the artist were disappointed when they met Pollock the drunk. 'You're all a bunch of horses' asses!' he used to bellow.

◀ A bar in Greenwich Village, the area in which Pollock drank with his fellow artists when he was in New York.

TIMELINE ▶

November 1950	Summer/Autumn 1951	Spring 1952	November 1952
Pollock starts drinking again. His fourth show at Betty Parsons is a great success.	Art News prints Namuth's photos and MoMA screens Namuth's film. Pollock exhibits his black paintings in his fifth show for Parsons.	'Jackson Pollock 1948-51' exhibition in Paris. Pollock included in MoMA's '15 Americans' exhibition.	Pollock's first show at Sidney Janis includes Blue Poles: Number 11, 1952 and Convergence: Number 10, 1952.

Number 14, 1951

enamel on canvas 146.4 x 269.2 cm Tate Gallery, London

Black paint for the blackest despair. From 1951, Pollock began to use enamel, which is much runnier and harder to control than oil paint. The black paintings are nightmare-like. Ghostly figures and faces with staring eyes seem to be hiding in the gaps between the poured black paint.

'Last year I thought, at last I'm above water from now on in – but things don't work that easily, I guess.'

Pollock, writing to Ossorio in January 1951

A tragic end

By 1953, Pollock was painting less and less and, for the first time in a decade, he did not have a solo show. He seemed unsure which direction to take with his painting.

Portrait and a Dream (opposite) splits the wide canvas into two distinct styles – figurative and abstract. On the right is a tortured head, perhaps a portrait of himself or Krasner, while the left is taken up with poured black enamel swirls.

In other works, too, Pollock goes back to earlier styles and hops between ideas. *Easter and the Totem*, for example, first shown in 1955, shares the bright palette and brushy, sparse style of the much earlier *Stenographic Figure* (see page 19).

SEPARATION

As Pollock's bouts of drinking became more frequent, Krasner despaired. In 1956, she suggested that they go away together to Europe, but Pollock was too depressed. Krasner flew to Europe alone and Pollock began an affair with a young New Yorker, Ruth Kligman.

On 11 August, Pollock got drunk and smashed his car into a tree, killing himself and a passenger, Edith Metzger. Kligman, also a passenger, was seriously injured.

▲ Pollock and Krasner in 1956. Pollock was scarcely painting any more, and his drinking bouts were taking their toll on the relationship.

▶ A 1950s Oldsmobile, similar to the one in which Pollock was killed.

FAST CARS

In 1949, as his fame increased, Pollock exchanged his old-fashioned Ford for a Cadillac convertible. He crashed it, drunk, in December 1951.

He crashed again in 1954 while travelling with fellow artist Franz Kline.

Pollock's final car was a green 1950 Oldsmobile convertible. He had swapped two of his black paintings for it.

TIMELINE ▶

1954	1955	Summer 1956	December 1956
Pollock included in '12 Peintres et Sculpteurs Americains Contemporains' exhibited in Paris, Zurich, Düsseldorf, Stockholm, Helsinki and Oslo.	Second Sidney Janis show. Pollock's end of the year show is a retrospective because he has few new works. He resumes therapy.	Krasner goes to Europe. Pollock starts an affair with Ruth Kligman. He dies in a car crash on 11 August. Krasner returns for his funeral.	MoMA's Pollock retrospective opens. It includes 35 paintings.

Portrait and a Dream, 1953
oil on canvas 148.6 x 342.2 cm Dallas Museum of Art

This painting splits neatly into two halves. The portrait on the right could be of Krasner, or Pollock himself.
Unlike the gloomy self-portrait at the beginning of his career (see page 8), this head is coloured with patches
of bright red and yellow, as well as darker tones. It was painted with brushes on an upright canvas.
On the left is what is inside the head – the 'dream' – a tangle of monochrome (black-only) connections
in poured paint which was created with the canvas flat on the floor.

'When you're painting out of your unconscious,
figures are bound to emerge.'

Jackson Pollock, interviewed in 1956

Pollock's legacy

Today, the house that Pollock and Krasner shared on Long Island is open to the public. Visitors can see inside his studio and look at the paint-spattered floor (see page 30).

The Pollock-Krasner Study Center also houses an important library of books and films about all the Abstract Expressionists. It organises talks about the life and work of Pollock and his contemporaries – and their impact on modern art.

DRIP PAINTINGS

Dripping was not a new idea when Pollock did it – or even new to him. In 1936 Pollock had seen Siqueiros splattering paint from a stick, as a way of coming up with ideas. Pollock knew that Hans Hofmann had dripped over his 1940 painting *Spring*. And he probably saw Max Ernst's oscillation paintings (made by swinging a tin of paint with a hole in it) at a 1942 Betty Parsons exhibition.

Pollock's drip paintings are important because the splatters were the actual meaning, the beginning and end, of what the paintings were about. Through those energetic tangles of paint, Pollock managed to express his tortured creativity on canvas. And that idea – that the painting process itself could be the subject of art – was so revolutionary that it is hard to think of any artist coming after Pollock who was not influenced by it.

▲ Inside the Pollock-Krasner House and Study Center.

Humanity Asleep, Julian Schnabel, 1982. The surface of the canvas is embedded with pieces of broken crockery and the paint is dull, thick and sludgy. Schnabel's raw, crude style looks abstract at first, but there is a figure on the right, as well as two faces fenced in at the centre.

PERFORMANCE ART

Performance art developed from Pollock's action painting. One of the people who took this a step further was the French artist Yves Klein (1928-62). He created his *Blue* paintings by making models cover themselves in blue paint and then, conductor-like, directing their movements on a huge canvas laid out on the floor.

SURFACE RICHES

Pollock showed how expressive the surface of a painting could be, too. In the 1980s, a new movement of expressive, abstract artists

arose. They were called the Neo-Expressionists, and included Anselm Kiefer (b.1945) and Georg Baselitz (b.1938) in Germany, Francesco Clemente (b.1952) in Italy, and Julian Schnabel (b.1951) and David Salle (b.1952) in the USA. Like Pollock, they

used wall-size canvases and very thick paint. Schnabel introduced personal elements into his paintings, just like Pollock did in *Full Fathom Five* (see page 29). 'I want my life to be embedded in my work… crushed into my painting, like a pressed car,' Schnabel said.

▶ Yves Klein in 1960, in front of two of his *Blue* paintings, created by naked, paint-covered women.

Summing up a human being

Krasner introduced Pollock to the critic Clement Greenberg in about 1942, saying 'He's going to be a great painter.' Greenberg replied, 'That's no way to sum up a human being.'

In the years that followed, the critic went further than anyone else in trying to sum up Pollock. Championing the artist established Greenberg's reputation. In turn, his reviews made Pollock famous, by helping others to understand what his paintings were all about.

◀ A Greenberg review in *The Nation* magazine, March, April 1945.

'Pollock's second one-man show at Art of This Century establishes him, in my opinion, as the strongest painter of his generation and perhaps the greatest to appear since Miró… He is not afraid to look ugly – all profoundly original art looks ugly at first.'

'Pollock points a way beyond the easel, beyond the mobile, framed picture, to the mural, perhaps – or perhaps not. I cannot tell.'

▲ Greenberg reviewing Pollock's fourth solo show (January 1947) in the magazine *The Nation*.

'The most powerful painter in contemporary America and the only one who promises to be a major one is a Gothic, morbid and extreme disciple of Picasso's Cubism and Miró's post-Cubism, tinctured also with Kandinsky and Surrealist inspiration. His name is Jackson Pollock.'

▲ Greenberg writing in the English magazine *Horizon* in October 1947.

TIMELINE ▶

1912	1936	1942	1944	1947
1912 Pollock is born on 28 January in Cody, Wyoming.	**1936** Pollock joins Siqueiros' experimental workshop.	**1942** *Birth* is in 'American and French Paintings'. Pollock and Krasner move in together. Art of This Century gallery opens. WPA Art Program disbanded.	**1944** MoMA buys *The She-Wolf*.	**1947** Pollock's fourth and last solo show at Art of This Century, before it closes in May.
1928 Pollock enrols at Manual Arts High School.	**1937** Pollock begins Jungian therapy.		**1945** Pollock's second solo show at Art of This Century. Pollock marries Krasner and they move to Springs.	**1948** Pollock shows his earliest drip paintings at Betty Parsons. He gives up alcohol, after treatment from his local GP, Edwin Heller.
1930 Pollock enrols at Art Students League.	**1938** Pollock is treated at Bloomingdale Asylum.	**1943** *Stenographic Figure* is in Art of This Century's 'Spring Salon for Young Artists'. In November, Pollock's first solo show opens there.	**1946** Pollock moves into his studio barn. His third solo show for Guggenheim opens in April. Pollock is included in the *Whitney Annual* for the first time.	
1935 Pollock joins the Federal Art Project (FAP) mural division.	**1941** Pollock is classified unfit for military service. Peggy Guggenheim arrives in New York.			

'Recently a formidably highbrow New York art critic hailed this brooding, puzzled-looking man as a major artist of our time and a fine candidate to become "the greatest American painter of the 20th century". Others believe that Jackson Pollock produces nothing more than interesting, if inexplicable, decorations. Still others condemn his pictures as degenerate and find them unpalatable as yesterday's macaroni...'

▲ From the article, 'Jackson Pollock: Is he the greatest living painter in the United States?' in *Life* magazine, 8 August 1949. The 'formidably highbrow' critic referred to was none other than Clement Greenberg.

'Pollock learned to control flung and dribbled paint almost as well as he could a brush; if accidents played any part, they were happy accidents, selected accidents...'

▲ From 'The Jackson Pollock Market Soars' by Clement Greenberg, first printed in *The New York Times Magazine* on 16 April 1961.

CLEMENT GREENBERG

Like his rival Harold Rosenberg, the American art critic Clement Greenberg (1909-94) made his name through his enthusiasm for the Abstract Expressionists. Rosenberg's favourite painter was Rothko; Greenberg's was Pollock.

Greenberg had studied at the Art Students League and Syracuse University. In 1942 he began writing reviews for *The Nation*, and quickly showed that he liked daring, uncompromising work.

Greenberg long outlived Pollock. He offered great encouragement to the next generation of American abstract painters, including Helen Frankenthaler (b.1928), Ellsworth Kelly (b.1923) and Frank Stella (b.1936). Greenberg coined the term Post-Painterly Abstraction to describe their work.

◀ Clement Greenberg photographed in his library.

1949	1950	1952	1955	1956
1949 Pollock holds two solo shows at Betty Parsons. The paintings are numbered, not named. In August *Life* magazine prints 'Jackson Pollock: Is he the greatest living painter in the United States?'.	**1950** MoMA buys *Number 1A, 1948*. Over the summer, Hans Namuth documents Pollock at work. In November, Pollock starts drinking again and his fourth show for Parsons opens. **1951** *Life* magazine prints 'Irascibles' photo. Pollock's last show at Parsons features black paintings.	**1952** Pollock moves to Sidney Janis Gallery. His first show includes *Blue Poles: Number 11, 1952* and *Convergence: Number 10, 1952*. **1954** Pollock's second show at Sidney Janis includes *Easter and the Totem, Portrait and a Dream* and *Unformed Figure*.	**1955** Pollock starts therapy in New York. He produces so few paintings that his third show for Sidney Janis includes many earlier works. He finishes his last two paintings.	**1956** Krasner goes to Europe. Pollock starts an affair with Ruth Kligman. He dies on 11 August, after driving his car into a tree when drunk. In December MoMA puts on a Pollock retrospective which includes 35 paintings.

Glossary

abstract: art that does not imitate the world around us. It is usually impossible to recognise objects, people or places in abstract art.

Abstract Expressionism: the name given to the work of several artists painting in different but related ways in New York in the 1940s and 50s. Their work is abstract, its subject being the actual process of painting.

action painting: a term coined by the critic Harold Rosenberg to describe a very 'active' painting style, for example, as used by Pollock in his drip paintings.

alcoholism: dependency on the drug alcohol.

archetype: a symbol or model of a particular idea or object.

automatism: the process of writing or drawing without thinking as a way of expressing unconscious thoughts.

collage: a picture made by pasting photographs, newspaper cuttings, string, labels and other objects on to a flat surface.

collective unconscious: according to Carl Jung, a shared store of stories and memories, buried deep in everyone's brain.

colour-field painting: a branch of Abstract Expressionism, in which artists used large expanses of colour to express themselves.

Communist: a supporter of the political system first suggested by Karl Marx (1818-83) under which everyone shares a country's goods and property.

composition: an artistic arrangement of parts of a painting or the subjects for a photograph.

Cubism: the name of an art movement based in Paris from about 1907, led by Pablo Picasso and Georges Braque. The Cubists painted multiple viewpoints of people or objects so they could all be seen at once.

detracting: taking away or diminishing.

gouache: opaque (milky) watercolours that have been mixed with water, honey and gum.

Great Depression: the global economic slump of the 1930s.

mural: a large painting on a wall.

Neo-Expressionism: an abstract art movement that began in the 1980s, using vigorous brushwork.

New Deal: US President Franklin Roosevelt's attempt to reduce the effects of the Great Depression by investing money in new public works projects, such as the Federal Art Program.

New York School: another name for the Abstract Expressionists, because the artists were mostly working in New York.

perspective: the art of suggesting three dimensions on a two-dimensional surface.

primitive art: art created by peoples outside the Western, 'civilised' world – for example by Native Americans or by African or Oceanic peoples.

psychological: to do with the mind.

Regionalism: a movement in American painting, mainly in the 1930s, that focused on depicting typical scenes from the American West.

reservation Indians: Native Americans who had been taken away from their ancestral lands and forced to live in enclosed areas of land, called reservations.

Surrealism: an intellectual movement that began in the 1920s, which tried to show the life of our unconscious minds and dreams. Its most famous artist is Salvador Dalí, but it also included writers and film-makers.

theosophy: a belief that one can know God through contact with spiritually gifted people.

therapy: a cure; often used to describe treatment for diseases of the mind.

unconscious: the most hidden part of someone's mind, where their deepest desires are stored.

Museums and galleries

Works by Pollock are exhibited in museums and galleries all around the world. Some listed here are devoted solely to Pollock, but most have a wide range of other artists' works on display.

Even if you can't visit any of these galleries yourself, you may be able to visit their websites. Gallery websites often show pictures of the artworks they have on display. Some of the websites even offer virtual tours which allow you to wander around and look at different paintings while sitting comfortably in front of your computer!

Most of the international websites detailed below include an option that allows you to view them in English.

INTERNET LINKS

Web Museum: Jackson Pollock
http://www.ibiblio.org/wm/paint/auth/pollock/

EUROPE

Centre National d'Art et de Culture Georges Pompidou
75191 Paris
cedex 04,
France
www.centrepompidou.fr

Museum Ludwig, Cologne
Bischofsgartenstrasse 1
D-50667 Cologne
Germany
www.museenkoeln.de/ludwig/

Peggy Guggenheim Collection
Palazzo Venier dei Leoni
701 Dorsoduro
30123 Venice
Italy
www.guggenheim-venice.it/english/

Tate Modern
Bankside
London SE1 9TG
www.tate.org.uk

USA

Albright-Knox Art Gallery
1285 Elmwood Avenue
Buffalo
NY 14222
www.akag.org

Art Institute of Chicago
111 Michigan Avenue
Chicago
IL 60603
www.artic.edu

Metropolitan Museum of Art
1000 Fifth Avenue
NY 10028
New York
www.metmuseum.org

The Museum of Fine Arts, Houston
1001 Bissonnet (at Main)
Houston
Texas 77005
www.mfah.org

The Museum of Modern Art
11 West 53rd Street
NY 10019
New York
www.moma.org
http://www.moma.org/exhibitions/pollock/website100/index.html

National Gallery of Art
4th Street and Constitution
Avenue NW
Washington DC 20565
www.si.edu/organiza/affil/natgal/start.html

Pollock-Krasner House and Study Center
830 Fireplace Road
East Hampton
NY 11937-1512
www.pkhouse.org

The Smithsonian Institution
Washington DC
www.si.edu

Solomon R Guggenheim Museum
1071 Fifth Avenue at 88th Street
NY 10128
New York
http://math240.lehman.cuny.edu/gugg/srgm.html

AUSTRALIA

National Gallery of Australia
Parkes Place
Canberra ACT 2601
Australia
www.nga.gov.au

Index